SUPERHEROES ARE EVERYWHERE

By Danielle Gallop

Illustrated by Sophia Badillo

About the Author

Danielle Gallop is happily married to Mike Gallop, Owner, and Operator of Twins BBQ and Tapville of Western CT. She is the VERY proud mother of two amazingly incredible adults, Kaia and Teja. Danielle and her family own and operate Honey Tree Preschools in CT, where, along with their Dream Team, they inspire lifelong learners and quality, lasting relationships. Danielle is also an Education Coordinator with the State of CT. Danielle loves spending time with friends, reading and attending book club, paddle boarding, and just about anything outdoors. She wrote this book to demonstrate that everyone is unique and wonderful in their own way. Her hope is that children (and adults) will find inspiration and self-worth in these pages.

About the Illustrator

Sophia Badillo, our 9-year-old illustrator, loves to draw. She is in 3rd grade where she enjoys coding, Spanish/English immersion, and excels in all her studies. She listens to all kinds of music and you can find her singing if there is music. She is the big sister to Dominick and her new baby brother Alexander. Sophia would like to be an author-illustrator when she grows up.

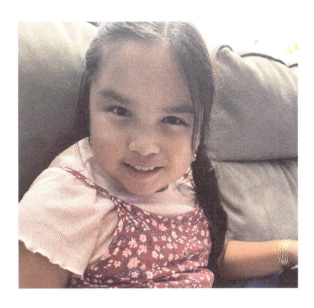

Acknowledgement

I would like to thank my daughters Kaia and Teja, all of the staff and children at Honey Tree, and Mike for inspiring me every single day! And, to Wendy who encouraged me to see this through. Surprise Ya'll!

Dedication

For my husband, Mike, who will forever be my superhero.

"Good Morning Class!" says Ms. Shoe
"Good Morning!" says the class.

"Today we are lucky enough to have a police officer visiting us!" Ms. Shoe says with a smile.
"Police are SUPERHEROES." yells Ava.
"Firemen are too!" Bailey adds.
"So are first responders" Callan shyly adds.
"…and doctors and nurses" shouts Davis.

"Superheroes are everywhere!"
Officer Evans tells the group.

Officer Evans tells the whole class what police do every day to keep the community safe and help all its members. When he finishes, the class cheers and waves goodbye.

It's time for snack. Freda cannot find her lunchbox. "I see it…. It's way down here." Garret, who is smaller than everyone in his class says. He wiggles his way under the cabinet and presents Freda with her lunchbox.

"You did it, Garret! You are the only person who could fit in there! Thank you!" Freda is delighted. "You are my superhero!" She tells him, and Garret, who usually feels shy because he is so small, sits with Freda for snack.

After snack, the class gets ready for recess. Hector cannot reach his jacket. "My mom put it way up there," he points to a hook way above the cubbies.

"Let me help you," says Imogen. She is the tallest one in the class and can reach his jacket easily.

"Thank you!" Hector rejoices. "That was so high! And it is chilly outside!" Imogen blushes, she usually tries not to stand out because being so tall makes her feel different.

"You are a superhero too! Do you want to play on my team? We are playing basketball." asks Hector. "Sure," says Imogen, surprised and happy to be included.

On the playground, the children have so much fun! After a little while, Jayden hears someone crying. He wheels himself over to the swings to find Kaia crying on the ground. Her knee is bleeding.

"Here," says Jayden, "hop-on! I will take you to the nurse." Kaia's tears stop and a smile appears. "Thank you! You are my superhero!" she says as Jayden takes her to the nurse.

When the children return to their classroom, it is time for music. Ms. Shoe picks Lia to sing for the class. Lia is new to the school and very shy. She doesn't talk to anyone in class and has yet to make friends. Lia begins to sing.

Her voice is beautiful. Marcus, another new addition to the class begins to dance! Nobody has ever done this before. Ms. Shoe starts to clap and before long the whole class is dancing and having so much fun. They all cheer for Lia and Marcus

"Thank you! You are both superheroes for making this so fun!" they say altogether. Each child is grinning from ear to ear with pleasure. Lia and Marcus are smiling too!

Their math lesson is next. Nia does not like math. She tries to hide behind her book so nobody can see her. Olivia leans over and asks Nia for help. Nia looks at Olivia's paper and sees her mistake – "just add a one."

Olivia is so grateful, "You are a lifesaver," Olivia tells her "my superhero!" Nia cannot help but laugh. "Maybe math is not so bad," she thinks.

Once math is over, Pheobe and Quinn ask to go to the bathroom. Ms. Shoe gives them a hall pass and off they go. On their way, they see a girl who looks lost. "Are you ok?" they ask. Rea stares up, trying to hide her sadness. "I am looking for the bathroom." she manages to say without crying.

"Come with us!" The two girls reply. "You are the best!" Rea replies "I would be lost without you! You guys are my superheroes!"

Later, at lunch, Silas drops his lunch on the floor.

Teja comes to the rescue, telling Mr. Unger, who asks the lunch helper to get Silas a new tray. "Thanks, Teja. I was so embarrassed. You are my superhero; I am really hungry – and I love tater-tots!"

Violet is missing when the class comes back from lunch. Wade thinks he may know where she is. He asks Ms. Shoe if he can help find Violet. "Of course!" she replies. And off he goes.

The rest of the class is getting ready for art when Xander spills paint all over his sweater. His face turns red and he puts his head down on the table. Yolanda quickly grabs some paper towels and helps him. He cannot save his sweater, but Zachary has one in his backpack.

Xander is so grateful to Yolanda and Zach. "You guys are my superheroes. Thanks!" He let's them know.

Just then, Wade comes back in to report that he has found Violet. She slipped when she was heading out of the lunchroom. Everything from her lunchbox went rolling down the hallway. Wade helped her get everything together and even carried her lunchbox back to class.

"Thank you, Wade! You are my superhero today!" exclaims Violet.

At the end of the day, Ms. Shoe asks the class about their day! Each child is so eager to share the nice things their friends did for them, and how happy it made them.

Ms. Shoe points out that the Officer Evans was right, there are SUPERHEROES EVERYWHERE!!!

Everyone looks around at their classmates and new friends. They all agree it is nice to be a superhero and to have people help you when you need it!

The End

Printed in the USA
CPSIA information can be obtained
at www.ICGtesting.com
JSHW071537100823
46152JS00003B/5